Emerging Use of Force Issues: Balancing Public and Officer Safety

Office of Community Oriented Policing Services (COPS): U.S. Department of Justice

The BiblioGov Project is an effort to expand awareness of the public documents and records of the U.S. Government via print publications. In broadening the public understanding of government and its work, an enlightened democracy can grow and prosper. Ranging from historic Congressional Bills to the most recent Budget of the United States Government, the BiblioGov Project spans a wealth of government information. These works are now made available through an environmentally friendly, print-on-demand basis, using only what is necessary to meet the required demands of an interested public. We invite you to learn of the records of the U.S. Government, heightening the knowledge and debate that can lead from such publications.

Included are the following Collections:

Budget of The United States Government
Presidential Documents
United States Code
Education Reports from ERIC
GAO Reports
History of Bills
House Rules and Manual
Public and Private Laws

Code of Federal Regulations
Congressional Documents
Economic Indicators
Federal Register
Government Manuals
House Journal
Privacy act Issuances
Statutes at Large

EMERGING USE OF FORCE ISSUES

Balancing Public and Officer Safety

Report from the International Association of Chiefs
of Police/COPS Office Use of Force Symposium

EMERGING USE OF FORCE ISSUES

Balancing Public and Officer Safety

Report from the International Association of Chiefs of Police/COPS Office
Use of Force Symposium

This project was supported by Grant Number 2005-HS-WX-K016 awarded by the Office of Community Oriented Policing Services, U.S. Department of Justice. The opinions contained herein are those of the author(s) and do not necessarily represent the official position or policies of the U.S. Department of Justice. References to specific agencies, companies, products, or services should not be considered an endorsement by the author(s) or the U.S. Department of Justice. Rather, the references are illustrations to supplement discussion of the issues.

The Internet references cited in this publication were valid as of the date of this publication. Given that URLs and websites are in constant flux, neither the author(s) nor the COPS Office can vouch for their current validity.

ISBN 978-1-935676-56-0

March 2012

Contents

Dear Colleagues:

Far too often the public's perception of the use of force by police is different from those who are in law enforcement. This perception is heavily influenced by a variety of factors, including depictions in the media, and exacerbated by the increasing power of social media. In today's age, incidents of use of force can create a false narrative for the public concerning the appropriateness of police actions, albeit one that is not statistically representative or supported by data.

In response to this complex environment impacting the critical relationship between police and the communities they serve, the International Association of Chiefs of Police (IACP) and the Office of Community Oriented Policing Services (COPS Office) recognize the importance of these issues, and the influence they can have on community trust. To further examine the intricacies surrounding police use of force, IACP and the COPS Office held a symposium to achieve consensus surrounding the core use of force issues, and to identify strategies that can be employed to address these issues.

We hope that these discussions and recommendations as presented in Emerging Use of Force Issues: Balancing Public and Officer Safety *will help your agency and community to work together to successfully navigate these issues.*

Sincerely,

Bernard K. Melekian, Director
Office of Community Oriented Policing Services

About the COPS Office

The Office of Community Oriented Policing Services (COPS Office) is the component of the U.S. Department of Justice responsible for advancing the practice of community policing by the nation's state, local, territory, and tribal law enforcement agencies through information and grant resources.

Community policing is a philosophy that promotes organizational strategies that support the systematic use of partnerships and problem-solving techniques, to proactively address the immediate conditions that give rise to public safety issues such as crime, social disorder, and fear of crime.

Rather than simply responding to crimes once they have been committed, community policing concentrates on preventing crime and eliminating the atmosphere of fear it creates. Earning the trust of the community and making those individuals stakeholders in their own safety enables law enforcement to better understand and address both the needs of the community and the factors that contribute to crime.

- The COPS Office awards grants to state, local, territory, and tribal law enforcement agencies to hire and train community policing professionals, acquire and deploy cutting-edge crime fighting technologies, and develop and test innovative policing strategies. COPS Office funding also provides training and technical assistance to community members and local government leaders and all levels of law enforcement. The COPS Office has produced and compiled a broad range of information resources that can help law enforcement better address specific crime and operational issues, and help community leaders better understand how to work cooperatively with their law enforcement agency to reduce crime. Since 1994, the COPS Office has invested nearly $14 billion to add community policing officers to the nation's streets, enhance crime fighting technology, support crime prevention initiatives, and provide training and technical assistance to help advance community policing.

- By the end of FY2011, the COPS Office has funded approximately 123,000 additional officers to more than 13,000 of the nation's 18,000 law enforcement agencies across the country in small and large jurisdictions alike.

- Nearly 600,000 law enforcement personnel, community members, and government leaders have been trained through COPS Office-funded training organizations.

- As of 2011, the COPS Office has distributed more than 6.6 million topic-specific publications, training curricula, white papers, and resource CDs.

COPS Office resources, covering a wide breath of community policing topics—from school and campus safety to gang violence—are available, at no cost, through its online Resource Information Center at www.cops.usdoj.gov. This easy-to-navigate website is also the grant application portal, providing access to online application forms.

About the IACP

The International Association of Chiefs of Police is the world's oldest, largest, and most innovative nonprofit membership organization of police executives, with more than 21,000 members in more than 100 countries. IACP's leadership consists of the operating chief executives of international, federal, state, and local agencies of all sizes.

Since 1893, the International Association of Chiefs of Police has been serving the needs of the law enforcement community. Throughout these past 100-plus years, IACP has continued to launch historically acclaimed programs, conducted ground-breaking research, and provided exemplary programs and services to our membership across the globe.

The association's goals are to advance the science and art of police services; to develop and disseminate improved administrative, technical, and operational practices and promote their use in police work; to foster police cooperation and the exchange of information and experience among police administrators throughout the world; to bring about recruitment and training in the police profession of qualified persons; and to encourage adherence of all police officers to high professional standards of performance and conduct.

Acknowledgments

The International Association of Chiefs of Police project staff would like to acknowledge the following individuals for their strong support of the development of this use of force report:

- The programmatic and financial support provided by the Office of Community Oriented Policing Services (COPS Office), in particular the guidance provided by Al Pearsall, Special Assistant to the Principal Deputy Director for the COPS Office. His in-depth understanding of use of force issues and his passion to see improvements made were critical factors in the success of this effort.

- The counsel and direction of the symposium planning group (see page 30 for complete list) who came together with the IACP and the COPS Office staff to design the symposium and identify achievable goals for that meeting.

- The subject matter expertise provided by the symposium participants (see page 31 for complete list). Their candid input and advice expressed at the symposium became the foundation for the content of this report. We are also in their debt for their subsequent review of the draft report to insure its completeness and accuracy.

The IACP thanks all of the above individuals for allowing us to explore the role of law enforcement leadership in the improvement of use of force policies, procedures, and training, and helping us arrive at the key observations and recommendations reported in this document.

Project Staff

IACP Executive Staff

Bart Johnson
Executive Director

James McMahon
Deputy Executive Director

John Firman
Director, Research Center
Co-Director, Use of Force Project

IACP Project Staff

Karita Belloni
Intern
Research Center

Lydia Blakey
IACP Fellow/Chief Inspector
U.S. Marshals Service

Scott Brien
Staff
Research Center

David H. Chipman
Principal Report Author, IACP Fellow
Special Agent, ATF

Carrie Corsoro
Coordinator
Research Center

Jenny Gargano
Staff
Research Center

Stephen Fender
Staff
Research Center

David Paulson
Staff, Information Technologies
Co-Director, Use of Force Project

COPS Office Project Program Officer

Al Pearsall
Special Assistant to the Principal
Deputy Director

Executive Summary

According to the Bureau of Justice Statistics, 40 million persons had contact with police during the most recent year for which data was gathered (2008). An estimated 776,000 (1.9 percent) of the 40 million contacted respondents reported the use or threatened use of force at least once during these contacts.

These facts stand in stark contrast to the public perception of the frequency and appropriateness of force used by the police. In large part, the public perception of police use of force is framed and influenced by the media depictions, which present unrealistic and often outlandish representations of law enforcement and the policing profession. Nightly, police dramas and news programs show officer-involved shootings, high speed chases, and trips to the morgue to recover microscopic evidence. These myths are further reinforced in popular books and film.

Yet data produced regularly by government agencies and researchers who analyze the actions of law enforcement argue against this "made for television" or "ripped from the headlines" narrative that has skewed the public ideas of law enforcement. These reports describe a reality of law enforcement with regards to use of force that starkly contradicts the public perception. As a result of these misconceptions, the public has raised questions regarding police use of force practices. In turn, law enforcement has raised concerns about the public's support of the public safety mission.

In response to this complex environment impacting the critical relationship between police and the communities they serve, the International Association of Chiefs of Police (IACP) in partnership with the Office of Community Oriented Policing Services (COPS Office) held a symposium that focused on police use of force. The primary goal of the meeting was to achieve consensus surrounding core use of force issues, identifying those topics of particular urgency, and proposing effective strategies that respond to the most critical areas of concern.

In preparation for the symposium law enforcement professionals, use of force experts, and use of force researchers were identified and told to expect they would examine a wide range of topics, to include:

- Current use of force issues and concerns of law enforcement leaders
- Use of force policy and training advancement over the past 5 years
- Recent use of force incidents or issues that have affected law enforcement approach
- Use of force litigation and risk management from a local agency perspective
- New and emerging research on use of force at the university and law enforcement level
- Concerns about use of force that merit further exploration and investigation

During the Use of Force symposium participant discussion clustered around topics that were grouped as pre-incident, point of incident, and post-incident variables (see Figure 1 on page 8).

Pre-Incident ➡	At Point of Incident ➡	Post-Incident ➡
◆ Review of policy effectiveness	◆ Internal Affairs investigation	◆ Accountability
◆ Leadership role	◆ Press management	◆ Dissemination of information
◆ Review of training effectiveness	◆ Criminal investigation	◆ Adjustments/improvements
◆ Community education	◆ Community outreach	◆ Policy upgrades
◆ Citizen input	◆ Agency transparency	◆ Training upgrades
◆ Utilization of accountability software		◆ Public forums/meetings to address incident
◆ Research		
◆ Existing standards/case law		

Figure 1. Use of Force Incident Continuum

Source: IACP symposium advisory group, created at the January 5, 2011 planning meeting

Recommendations Summary

This publication presents a summary of discussions that took place during the Use of Force Symposium, key findings identified by the group, and recommendations for further action. The following suggested actions are systemic and would require funding support and collaboration between the IACP, the COPS Office, and any number of more private or public organizations to achieve successful completion. To further the good work done at the symposium, IACP and the COPS Office will be discussing the following recommendations shortly to determine possible courses of action to implement them:

- Develop a model communications strategy for law enforcement on the topic of use of force

- Develop a national media guide to inform the public regarding the necessity to use appropriate force in furtherance of public safety

- Develop a sustainable online resource library detailing programs and summaries of approaches that have proven to build better relationships between police and their communities

- Propose national use of force reporting standards

- Collect data and conduct annual national use of force analysis

- Conduct evaluation of use of force issues for the mid-size and small police agency

- Charge a single government sponsored entity with responsibility for disseminating real-time data describing violence directed at police

- Develop and fund a use of force management institute for police leaders

- Develop use of force management publication for city/town or municipal governance

- Survey to determine nationally the current spectrum of use of force training

- Develop model in-service use of force training

- Validate use of force in-service training in pilot departments

- Survey to evaluate the use of force mindset of police

- Support efforts such as the Department of Justice's Officer Safety and Wellness Group, IACP's National Center for the Prevention of Violence Against the Police (NCPVAP) and the FBI's Law Enforcement Officer Killed and Assaulted (LEOKA) program to collect, evaluate, discuss, and publish real-time, data that speaks to trends in violence directed against police

I. Introduction and Background

The Environment

Law enforcement faces innumerable challenges created by the current environment, particularly with regards to use of force. The public perception of the frequency and appropriateness of force used by the police is framed and influenced largely by the media depictions. Media has become saturated with unrealistic and outlandish representations of law enforcement and the policing profession. Nightly, police dramas and news programs depict officer-involved shootings, high speed chases, and trips to the morgue to recover microscopic evidence, while these myths are also reinforced in popular books and film. Data produced regularly by government agencies and researchers who analyze the actions of law enforcement argue against this "made for television" or "ripped from the headlines" narrative that has skewed the public ideas of law enforcement. These reports describe a reality of law enforcement with regards to use of force that starkly contradicts the public perception. As a result of these isolated incidents the public has raised questions regarding police use of force practices. In turn, law enforcement has raised concerns about the public's support of the public safety mission.

In response to this complex environment impacting the critical relationship between police and the communities they serve the International Association of Chiefs of Police (IACP) in partnership with the Office of Community Oriented Policing Services (COPS Office) held a symposium that focused on police use of force. This publication summarizes key use of force issues identified by subject matter experts in the field who were invited to participate in the symposium, and proposes effective strategies that respond to the most critical areas of concern.

The Facts

According to the Department of Justice, Bureau of Justice Statistics (BJS) we know many facts about law enforcement, in particular police operations and use of force practices. The most recent *Census of State and Local Law Enforcement Agencies, 2008* reports that there are 765,000 sworn officers employed in the United States. BJS has also produced data in their publication *Contacts between Police and the Public, 2008*, which attempts to estimate the frequency by which police use force in furtherance of their duties. BJS determined that 40 million persons had contact with police during 2008. An estimated 776,000 (1.9 percent) of the 40 million contacted respondents reported the use or threatened use of force at least once during these contacts. This report reveals a striking disconnect between public perception and reality—the public is led to believe through the media that law enforcement uses force during every tour of duty, when the reality is most officers never use or threaten the use of force during an entire calendar year. These statistics suggest that use of force by police is infrequent and that inappropriate use of force or negative force related outcomes are relatively rare events.

Where there is little debate among police leadership and members of the community is in the fact that the use of force by police results in public attention. According to Robert K. Olsen, the former Minneapolis Police Chief, in the Police Executive Research Forum (PERF) press release titled "PERF to Identify Best Practices in Police Use of Force and Managing Mass Demonstrations" from February 12, 2004, the use of force is "the single most volatile issue facing police departments." He noted that "just one use of force incident can dramatically alter the stability of a police department and its relationship with a community." Today, in the age of internet communications, news of incidents instantly becomes viral with this rapid sharing of information. A department's relationship with its community can easily be impacted by the actions of an officer in a department thousands of miles away.

The Purpose of a Symposium

The IACP recognizes the importance of continual research and evaluation of police use of force issues and believes findings from systematic and routine inquiry will inform model policies and procedures within the law enforcement community. As the risks to communities change, so do law enforcement responses to mitigate these threats. In recent years, technological advances in police equipment have provided additional use of force options for the front line officer while also generating the need for a new cycle of research and evaluation. Findings from extensive study and evaluation of use of force issues help law enforcement officials make fact-based decisions relating to use of force policy as well as improve communications with the public.

In an effort to focus future research and policy development, the IACP partnered with the COPS Office to organize a symposium of law enforcement and experts in the field to assess the current landscape of use of force issues. Subject matter experts representing diverse constituencies within the criminal justice system were invited to participate in a day-long meeting. An environment was created to foster open and frank discussion on a wide range of highly sensitive topics. The primary goals of the meeting were to learn core use of force issues, identify topics of particular urgency, document differences in opinion where they may exist, and propose effective strategies that respond to the most critical areas of concern.

In preparation for the symposium, law enforcement professionals, use of force experts, and use of force researchers were identified to participate, and asked to expect to examine a wide range of topics, including:

- Current use of force issues and concerns of law enforcement leaders
- Use of force policy and training advancement over the past 5 years
- Recent use of force incidents or issues that have affected law enforcement approach
- Use of force litigation and risk management from a local agency perspective
- New and emerging research on use of force at the university and law enforcement level
- Concerns about use of force that merit further exploration and investigation

This publication presents a summary of discussions that took place during the Use of Force Symposium, key findings identified by the group, and recommendations for further action.

Use of Force Incident Continuum

In examining police use of force issues it is advantageous to view the **incident** with a broad perspective rather than limiting the focus at the moment force is used. Actions taken or not taken **pre-incident** can have a significant influence on use of force decisions by the officer. Actions taken **post-incident** can also impact the future uses of force equally as those decisions prior to the event.

Pre-Incident variables are typified by a systematic approach by which leadership manages the use of force within an agency. Training, assessment, tracking, early-warning systems, community outreach, external relations, case law and research would be further examples of the categories of issues that may influence uses of force by officers within the **pre-incident** environment.

Incident variables include officer use of force decisions, suspect use of force decisions, and all relevant incident circumstances. Subsequent to the actual use of force and still part of the **incident** component of the continuum, a series of actions may be triggered, including agency transparency when discussing the incident, community outreach, press management, and internal or criminal investigative actions.

Post-Incident variables include systems of accountability and review that lead to changes in policy and training, or that may frequently be communicated via "after action" or "lessons learned" reports. Long-term and strategic communication to inform and influence the public reaction to incidents may be considered **post-incident**, as well as appropriate coordination with governing bodies with respect to liability and criminal culpability in those instances when excessive force was used.

During the Use of Force symposium, participant discussion clustered around topics that were identified as pre-incident, incident, and post-incident variables. Besides transparency with respect to details regarding actual use of force incidents, experts believed that actions taken prior to incidents and actions taken following incidents should be the focus of future IACP/COPS Office activities.

Use of Force 2001 to 2011

In 2001, the IACP, in collaboration with the Bureau of Justice Statistics and the National Institute of Justice, published *Police Use of Force in America*, which documented findings from the National Police Use of Force Database project initiated in 1995. The database was created in response to the Violent Crime Control and Law Enforcement Act of 1994 and represented the first substantial national aggregation of state, county, and local law enforcement use of force data. As a result of this landmark study 177,215 use of force incidents and 8,082 use of force complaints from 1991–2000 were examined.

Many guiding standards resulted from this systematic evaluation of use of force incidents. In order to ensure uniformity in reporting of incidents, IACP defined force as, **"that amount of effort required by police to compel compliance from an unwilling subject."** Excessive force was defined as, **"the application of an amount and/or frequency of force greater than that required to compel compliance from a willing or unwilling subject."** For the purposes of the 2001 publication, reports of excessive force that were investigated and sustained were considered excessive. Some organizations have rightfully commented that for some members of the public the mere presence of police can be construed as a use of force. Others may also argue that an internal departmental investigation of an officer's use of force lacks the independence necessary to obtain an unbiased assessment of the level of force used.

The IACP study also attempted to characterize trends in the use of force, uncovering many interesting facts, especially with regard to the impact of new deadly or non deadly technologies on policing. In 1999, the most common force used by officers was physical force. The use of chemical force, primarily *Oleoresin Capsicum* (pepper spray) products, was greater than the totals for electronic, impact, and firearms force combined. Throughout the years of study it was determined that as the use of chemical force increased by police, the reliance by officers on the use of firearm force decreased. This clearly suggests that by providing police with an array of deadly and non-deadly technologies they can perform their duties effectively while limiting harm to members of the community.

By 2005, the IACP recognized that once again, breakthroughs in technology were significantly influencing the method by which police deploy non-lethal force in furtherance of their mission. *Electro-Muscular Disruption Technology*, an IACP publication funded through a grant by the National Institute of Justice (NIJ), outlined a nine-step deployment strategy for departments who had decided to arm officers with state of the art non-lethal weapons such as the TASER®. At the time, 5,000 police departments had already chosen to issue Electronic Control Weapon (ECW) devices to officers.

By 2010, researchers on behalf of NIJ reported in *A Multi-Method Evaluation of Police Use of Force Outcomes: Final Report to the National Institute of Justice* that based on current industry estimates, ECW devices could be found in more than 11,500 police agencies nationwide. Presently, a majority of law enforcement agencies have adopted Conducted Energy Device (CED) (formerly ECW) technology as a use of force option for their agencies.

Use of Force Symposium May 4, 2011

During a daylong exchange of ideas, interactive polling, and debate concerning present and future needs of the policing profession, participants spoke to a variety of topics. For ease of digesting the most significant points of discussion, the themes have been organized in five major areas.

- Public Perception
- Getting at the Facts
- Managing Use of Force: A Chief's Duty
- Officer Training: After the Academy
- Officer Mindset

II. Public Perception

The public's perception of police use of force was a topic of concern for many symposium participants. When polled, only 4 of 36 symposium attendees believed that citizens were objective when evaluating use of force incidents. One in 10 had confidence that the public would examine the facts and circumstances unique to each individual incident. The remaining participants were divided in their beliefs. By a 3 to 1 majority, participants asserted that a bias against police existed, as compared to a minority who found that a bias in favor of police was typically present.

There was consensus that police leadership was responsible for educating the public and concern that the failure to adopt a proactive national communications strategy hindered police efforts to speak with clarity on the issue. In the absence of a cohesive fact-based message the media and other constituencies are left to frame the topic, which often results in sensationalizing incidents or driving the agenda of various special interest groups. As a result, police officials react to stories framed by others, rather than proactively communicating information within the framework of a unified national theme. Nearly two-thirds of participants believed that police did a poor job conveying information to the public regarding use of force incidents.

> Citizen Police Academies are excellent opportunities to help citizens move from misperceptions to full understanding of the complex nature of use of force.
>
> — Al Pearsall
> *Special Assistant to the Principal Deputy Director*
> Office of Community Oriented Policing Services

Participants were sensitive to the fact that the success of any future communications strategy was directly related to the level of trust existing between police and the public at the national and, most importantly, the local levels. As such, attendees understood that it was critical that any previous history involving the inappropriate use of force had to be acknowledged. Equally important was maintaining sensitivity to the various harms resulting from this unacceptable conduct and making clear statements necessary to ensure that leadership is not perceived as attempting to minimize the severity of the breach of the public trust.

It was suggested that a fundamental component of the communications message would be the use of common terms. Thirty-one of 34 symposium participants acknowledged that no common language existed for talking about use of force between police and the communities they serve. For example discussions of reasonable versus unreasonable uses of force were preferred as compared to debates over excessive force. Participants felt that misconceptions concerning the appropriateness of the level of force used by police could be often tied to how incidents were discussed. A significant piece of any communications strategy is to explain to the public why the police may employ force at a level greater than the force being used against the officer, and why this is appropriate

There is a large body of case law that permits the police to use force that is reasonably necessary to overcome the force used against them. The public often perceives that force as excessive when it is not.

— Philip Broadfoot, *Chief of Police*
Danville Police Department

and not excessive. Unlike a professional hockey fight where a player would be severely sanctioned for using his stick instead of his fist, an officer is expected and trained to deploy weapons such as a baton, pepper spray, or Taser to counter an offender determined to fight an officer. Use of these technologies is certainly considered a justified, reasonable, and appropriate use of force by an officer sworn to uphold the law and maintain public safety, and is an important action to minimize injury to both officers and suspects.

Participants were supportive of a variety of programs focused on developing better relationships between the police, the public, the media, and special interest groups. Citizen academies and ride along programs were suggested as vehicles by which participants would be provided an opportunity to better grasp the complexities and realities of being a law enforcement officer. These inclusive activities serve the critical function of making law enforcement policy and practice transparent. Youth programs in school, other extra curricula activities, and events were identified as opportunities to form a positive view of policing at an early age. Focused interactions and relationship building with specific constituencies aimed at developing trust and good will were seen as strategic necessities in anticipation for the need to respond quickly to contain the fall-out from use of force incidents in the future. In furtherance of influencing the public's view of the individual officers, it was also suggested that efforts be made to monitor and positively influence the demeanor of officers towards the public they serve. It was suggested that the everyday attitude of officers during the course of their routine activities has as great an influence on public perception as actual uses of force.

RECOMMENDATIONS:

▶ **DEVELOP** a model communications strategy for law enforcement on the topic of use of force.

▶ **DEVELOP** a national media guide to inform the public regarding the dangers of policing and the necessity to use appropriate force in furtherance of public safety.

▶ **DEVELOP** a sustainable online resource library detailing programs and summaries of approaches that have proven to build better relationships between police and their communities.

III. Getting at the Facts

Stemming from discussions regarding law enforcement's role in informing the public, concern was raised about police leadership's true understanding of current trends and statistics regarding the use of force landscape. Several participants challenged the assumption made by other attendees that police leaders had a firm grasp of the present use of force environment as well as accurate statistics relative to the dangerousness of policing today as compared to historical data. The differences in opinion were most profound when the views of academics, front line officers, and participants supporting police administration were contrasted with those expressed by chiefs of police and command officials. Similar differences were witnessed based on the size of the agency represented, as issues relating to use of force in large urban cities did not always align with issues experienced by mid-size and smaller departments. Supportive of this lack of consensus were the results of a survey where participants disagreed over a fundamental question regarding the trend in the rate of use of force incidents. Eight of 34 participants believed that use of force incidents had decreased, while 6 of 34 suspected that use of force incidents had increased. The majority estimated that force trends had remained the same. It was evident that local views and personal experience most influenced perception as to the overall state of use of force.

> Before we go out and educate people on use of force we need to educate ourselves.
>
> — Dr. Geoffrey Alpert, *Professor*
> University of South Carolina

Participants agreed that the collection and analysis of use of force data varied widely and that this challenge was likely to continue if not worsen as a result of the economic downturn. In departments forced to downsize, administrative positions traditionally charged with data collection are often the first to be eliminated. As a result, it was suspected that use of force data collection and analysis was currently the province of mostly larger departments. Concerns were also expressed regarding the applicability of findings born from big city data analysis to mid-size and smaller agencies.

Some participants believed that various departments collected use of force data in line with standards established by the Commission for Accreditation of Law Enforcement Agencies (CALEA) or other model reporting protocols. Others described data collection in line with state legislation and consent decrees. There was consensus, however, that for those departments who collected the data, most failed to analyze the data and/or use it for policy development or training purposes. The majority of departments had no policies or procedures in place that mandated annual analysis and reporting.

> So often after an event someone uses statistics to show what we should have known. We need to understand our history employing basic trend and pattern analysis before critical incidents occur.
>
> — Louis Dekmar, *Chief of Police*
> City of LaGrange

> We have a good understanding of larger departments but not the conditions and situations that impact smaller and medium agencies.
>
> — Dr. Geoffrey Alpert, *Professor*
> University of South Carolina

In response to the current use of statistics to inform public discussion on force trends, some participants were suspect of the "facts" that were purported. Participants speculated that a reliance on year to year comparisons is a function of reporting now common place in departments employing COMPSTAT. As such, data can be heavily influenced by periodic spikes not uncommon when measuring occurrences within small data sets such as officers feloniously killed in the line of duty. Some identified a void of more traditional multi-year historical statistical examinations readily available to inform leadership and members of the public regarding recent trends. These same participants expressed concern that the void has been filled by various experts and policy advocates expressing their point of view, rather than sharing facts, regarding current highly publicized and emotionally charged events.

> The perception is that chiefs know about use of force in their departments, but the reality is they often do not. When we come in afterward to ask for data to explain to a jury, it is almost impossible to obtain.
>
> — Steven Ijames, *Major (Ret.)*
> Springfield Police Department

It was suggested that much work should be done within the behavioral science communities to explore how police respond to deadly encounters. The belief was expressed that the police profession and the public at large do not fully understand myriad of factors that contribute to a typical use of force incident. It was posited that we often do not fully appreciate the complexities involved when an officer makes a decision to use force in relation to a critical incident.

RECOMMENDATIONS:

▶ **PROPOSE** National Use of Force reporting standards.

▶ **COLLECT** data and conduct annual National Use of Force analysis.

▶ **CONDUCT** evaluation of use of force issues for the mid-size and small police agency.

▶ **CHARGE** a single government sponsored entity with responsibility for collection, analysis, and dissemination of real-time data describing violence directed at police.

IV. Managing Use of Force: A Chief's Duty

Symposium participants were clearly cognizant of the varied responsibilities charged to leaders within police organizations. Specifically, during a downturn economy, fiscal emergencies and retention of the personnel required to meet mission goals were recognized as challenging tasks for any focused public safety official. Despite this environment, management of a police department's application of force in furtherance of its operations was understood to be every chief's fundamental responsibility.

Participants suggested that the gold standard of use of force management is a leader who possesses complete awareness of the use of force culture within his or her department and knowledge of the attitudes held by all officers to include those assigned to patrol, those charged with training, as well as those functioning within specialty assignments. Participants representing city management acknowledged that the vast majority of public officials have no law enforcement experience. As a result, an able use-of-force-focused police leader in service of the mayor or city manager would proactively establish a risk-based dialogue with city executives so that critical information regarding the potential implications of use of force incidents would be understood. Police leaders should in fact seek up-front support for investments in police training and equipment in lieu of post incident funding to offset legal judgments or settlements at a later date. A progressive city should view a highly resourced and trained police force as the appropriate cost of doing business rather than using public funds to establish an annual line item for legal settlements.

> I think what we are talking about is an affirmative obligation for police to manage use of force, not just to explain a particular incident to the public.
>
> — Merrick Bobb, *Director*
> Police Assessment Resource Center

Members of the symposium were clear that chiefs need to ensure that the level of competency and knowledge surrounding the appropriate use of force has been received and retained by officers. Leaders should set a high bar for professionalism and expect that use of force decisions would mature through experience and not degrade as the length of time from police academy graduation increases. Chiefs should be intimately aware of the culture surrounding in-service training within their departments to ensure that the highest level training is being offered.

Chiefs not only have to ensure that use of force data is being collected by their department but that it is collected in a format that it is useful for supervisors to drive decision making. Intelligence-led and evidence-based policing models not only drive better police work and targeting of crime problems, but also are approaches that improve decision making. Properly managed data can be the backbone of an early warning system that identifies at risk officers, dangerous activities, and policy gaps that require immediate mitigation.

City managers tend to know little about law enforcement. In an analysis of 9,000 members, only a handful had prior law enforcement experience.

— Leonard Matarese, *Director*
International City/County Management Association

Leaders also warned that the level of inexperience in dealing with critical use of force incidents should not be underestimated. Statistics suggest that use of force by police is infrequent and the inappropriate use of force or negative force related outcomes are a relatively rare event. However, each year a number of chiefs will have to respond to critical incidents when their officers have been killed, a suspect has been killed, or incidents occur that call into question the professionalism of certain officers. A chief must be prepared for this possibility and possess the confidence to take swift and decisive action. A chief's standing in the eyes of the public can be impacted by a single response to a critical incident.

For chiefs who are committed to preparing for a critical incident involving use of force issues, highly specialized training is essential. For example, table top exercises in partnership with other key players such as the city manager, command staff, public information officers, Department of Justice officials, and trusted partners within the media, police union, and public interests groups can be useful. Such exercises can simulate the type of pressures generated during a real crisis. Crafting a post-incident protocol in partnership with this group that fits the norms of unique communities and departmental policies and procedures would be invaluable as a guide during a real incident. Communication strategies that inform the public while maintaining the confidence of front line officers who require the chief's support require planning in advance, and should not be addressed for the first time during an emotionally charged event.

RECOMMENDATIONS:

▶ **DEVELOP** Use of Force Management Institute for Police Leaders.

▶ **DEVELOP** Use of Force Management publication for City Officials.

V. Officer Training: After the Academy

As recognized by symposium participants, there is much about the use of force topic that we do not understand, but much that we suspect. What we do know for certain is that leaders have a professional obligation to train law enforcement to the fullest degree in order to ensure officer safety as well as public safety. Symposium participants also clearly believed that police professionals were falling short in their duty to train officers. Fourteen of 33 attendees believed that use of force training "insufficiently" prepared police, while only a single attendee believed that officers were "very well" prepared.

Many symposium participants shared a concern that in-service trainings have not been validated in the same rigorous fashion as academy training, and that the level of accountability is far different for officers when approaching in-service training—as they do not fear failure or loss of job based on poor performance during these exercises. Performance related action against employees as a result of non-compliance with in-service training guidelines is much more complex than similar issues encountered during academy training. Employees at the academy stage have yet to be certified or have only been hired conditionally and are within a probationary period where corrective action can be taken aggressively.

Symposium participants shared many concerns regarding the training environment. Their primary concerns centered on fears that a downturn economy would impact the ability to train. Simultaneously, they felt there has never been a more important time to be properly trained. Some chiefs felt that due to public perception and fear of lawsuits, some officers were inadvertently being trained to return fire only when fired upon rather than using that force reasonably necessary to prevent injury or death.

> I've supported in-service training across the country and while it is a critical training delivery opportunity, officers are often distracted or disinterested. This problem is confirmed as I read depositions for officers being sued. There is no evidence they learned anything except how to shoot. If we want consistency we need to know they know what they are being trained on and validate that training.
>
> — Steven Ijames, *Major (Ret.)*,
> Springfield Police Department

Some leaders suggested that insurance companies may be appropriate funding sources, or at a minimum advocates, to influence the city officials who make tough financial decisions for their communities.

A number of participants built upon the themes surrounding the chief's duty to manage use of force within the department. Participants suggested that video and audio recordings should be used more routinely as tools to manage and train officers. Use of audio/video will allow first-line supervisors to critique use of tactics or communication meant to manage conflict. Other participants were concerned that too much technology and too many choices in weapons systems degraded an officer's operational awareness and slowed reaction times. Some participants were concerned that more training needed to be focused on communication and command presence. Concern was shared that, later in their careers, officers often did not look prepared, while younger officers relied too much on physicality as opposed to using verbal tactics to deescalate and mitigate confrontational situations.

Participants questioned if training had become ineffective because it was based on what an officer could not do rather than a positive format focused on what an officer could do or in fact must do with respect to the use of force. In considering further changes to the framework by which training has been conducted, participants suggested that survivors should be interviewed more comprehensively, and training needed to be focused on situations based in reality as opposed to training that simply provided certification. There was consensus that firearm and/or force training needed to transition from the standard qualification of using age old static point and shoot courses. For training to be relevant, it was deemed essential to transition to tactical courses that replicate real encounters, requiring a choice between a variety of use of force options during stressful simulations as well as closely supervised tactical training environments.

Participants were briefed on the National Center for the Prevention of Violence Against the Police (NCPVAP), a collaborative effort between the International Association of Chiefs of Police and the Bureau of Justice Assistance. The mission of the National Center is to explore data currently collected detailing felonious assaults against police and to share findings with law enforcement in order to reduce officer deaths and injuries. Recently, the National Center revealed details regarding an examination of 10 years of Law Enforcement Officers Killed and Assaulted (LEOKA) data published by the FBI in an effort to examine use of force in response to deadly encounters. Researchers suspected that there would be value in examining responses to incidents through the lens of the years of service of the officer.

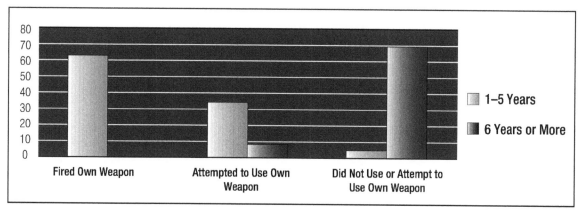

Figure 2. Weapon Use by Years of Service, 2000–2009

Source: IACP's National Center for the Prevention of Violence Against the Police. Author: Stephen Fender, IACP Project Coordinator

The FBI reports there were 187 officers with 5 years of service or less and 339 officers with 6 years of service or more that were killed in the line of duty during the past 10 years. When examining the group of less experienced officers (with 5 years or fewer on the job) the NCPVAP found that during the incident 63.1 percent fired their weapon, 33.2 percent attempted to fire their weapon, and 3.7 percent did not make an attempt. Of those more experienced officers (with 6 years or service or more) not a single one of 339 officers fired their weapon while only 8.6 percent were documented to have even made an attempt (see Figure 2). The National Center will continue to conduct in-depth examinations of these kinds of data to determine their value to police policy and training.

RECOMMENDATIONS:

▶ **SURVEY** to determine nationally the current spectrum of Use of Force Training

▶ **DEVELOP** model In-Service Use of Force Training

▶ **VALIDATE** Use of Force In-Service Training in Pilot Departments

VI. Officer Mindset

The IACP and COPS Office Use of Force Symposium created a safe environment for participants to have candid conversations, share concerns, and seek affirmations for personal observations. Symposium demographics were heavily weighted toward tenured experts in leadership positions, talking about use of force from a leadership perspective. Given that the vast majority of uses of force are employed by front line officers, symposium participants were reflecting on secondary observations concerning the actions of others or recalling their own experiences.

What officers think about the use of force and the factors that influence this decision are complex and unique to every officer. Understanding these dynamics is essential before attempts are made to manage, train, or otherwise influence an officer's use of force. Further research that supports a more comprehensive understanding of the officer's mindset is essential before moving forward.

> I think the response that I'm not going to do my job because someone will object is despicable. Part of being a police professional is using appropriate force and learning to deal with criticism.
>
> — Merrick Bobb, *Director*
> Police Assessment Resource Center

During the symposium discussion on officer mindset, concerns were voiced on a number of subjects that have enormous ramifications to the use of force conversation. The first centered on law enforcement's perception concerning the level of violence directed against them as police. The spike in police fatalities that had occurred earlier in 2011 was noted. Many assumed that policing had never been more dangerous and appropriate action needed to be taken to defend police against an increased risk of injury and death. Others offered a different perspective, raising concerns about an alarmist response that could result in the over-reaction of police and a retreat from community oriented policing.

Participants voiced concerns that officers were often in a state of paralysis when it came to the use of force because of the unintended consequences of department use of force reporting requirements, outside review boards, internal affairs actions, liability concerns, and the ramification of criticism from outside constituencies.

> We need to focus on the balance of officer and public safety—and to ensure that balance. When any citizen is injured or killed, and improper force is suspected, it must be fully investigated.
>
> — Al Pearsall, *Special Assistant to the Principal Deputy Director*
> Office of Community Oriented Policing Services

> The recent police deaths are tragic but the most violent year for police occurred in 1971. We need to take this data and examine it historically rather than take it raw and think we are under siege. Without proper analysis there is fear that is unwarranted.
>
> — Louis Dekmar, *Chief of Police*
>   City of LaGrange

From this discussion it appears critical that a variety of questions should be asked of front line officers. This inquiry could include questions regarding officer's fears or apprehension to use force, their sense of the relative dangerousness of their jobs, the perception of members of the community and how they are viewed by the community, their beliefs about the supportiveness of police leadership, the consistency of their actual reporting of use of force incidents, the types of use of force reporting and procedures in their department, their views on training at the academy and in-service, as well as their views regarding their role as police in the community they serve.

Participants collectively voiced a desire to have access to the facts concerning the actual violence currently leveled at police. When the environment is perceived as more dangerous, police leaders are likely to support increasing levels of force to protect officers. Evidence of this trend can already be found in academia and government reports. Eastern Kentucky University criminologist Peter Kraska has published statistics suggesting that SWAT deployments in the United States have increased from 3,000 in 1980 to nearly 45,000 during 2007. In Maryland, where reporting the use of tactical teams is required by law, SWAT teams were used over 1,600 times during a 1-year period ending in June of 2010.[1] It is clear that leaders base force decisions on the prevailing crime and community context within their jurisdiction. Clearly, to maintain the trust with the community, belief about dangerousness must be congruent with the facts based on solid analysis of verifiable data, which in turn should be shared with the public.

Symposium members also struggled to characterize the actual and appropriate mindset of front line officers today. Despite an active conversation regarding the current feelings of front line officers, little consensus could be made. Leaders expressed a strong need for information concerning the actual threat of violence, and the state of mind of their front line officers. They noted that this need was immediate and could not wait for findings from lengthy multi-year research efforts. A sense of urgency was shared concerning the need for accurate data as well as the analysis required to understand these baseline factors before pushing forward in many of the areas addressed during the symposium.

RECOMMENDATIONS:

▶ **SURVEY** to evaluate the Use of Force Mindset of Police Officers

▶ **SUPPORT** efforts such as LEOKA and the National Center for Prevention of Violence Against the Police to collect, evaluate, and publish in real-time, data that speaks to trends in violence directed against police.

---

1.   Kris Coronado. 2011. "Unnecessary Roughness." *Washingtonian Magazine.* April.

VII. Conclusion

The IACP/COPS Use of Force Symposium helped to identify critical issues and innovative recommendations to address them. Most of the recommendations are focused at the national policy and funding levels. Now that this report is in dissemination, IACP and the COPS Office will begin discussing how to maintain momentum to ensure these recommendations are implemented and, in particular, how to engage a broader spectrum of both public and private law enforcement leaders to support further work in this field.

While these national-level discussions proceed, it is equally urgent that local law enforcement leaders take immediate steps to strengthen their agencies' approach to all aspects of use of force policy. As always, local leaders need not wait for major national-level activities to emerge; rather they can use their authority to address issues—when necessary—with immediacy. Looking at this report's recommendations through the local lens, the following is a set of suggested actions that may be of critical value if addressed:

- **Officer mindset:** Hold regular briefings at both the command and officer level to fully understand how officers think about force issues, including policy adherence, liability, internal force reviews, public perceptions, and suspects' use of force against officers. Their perceptions will have a direct impact on how they use or do not use force.

- **Force policy and training:** Conduct a review of force policies, looking at both state and local policy models, to ensure currency and comprehensiveness. Revise and enhance all policies as needed. Make sure all use of force training is entirely consistent with policy and it both reinforces and further articulates policy intent.

- **Force reporting:** Review current use of force reporting policies in the context of both state and national models, and update or revise those policies as appropriate or needed. Proactively use that data to conduct annual use of force reviews that can influence policy and training enhancement.

- **Communications strategy:** Review local communications strategies to ensure preparedness and transparency in the event of a use of force incident that necessitates public commenting. On a regular basis, seek opportunities to gauge public perception on general use of force issues, absent of any recent incident.

- **Media:** Work with local media to educate them on use of force policy, training, and practices so they view and report on future incidents in an informed, contextual manner. Share that education with governing body leaders so they have the same contextual information as they review use of force incidents.

As symposium participants stated in Chapter IV, "the gold standard of use of force management is a leader who possesses complete awareness of the use of force culture within his or her department and knowledge of the attitudes held by all officers...." Taking action on the above items will enable local law enforcement leaders to gain critical information and perspective on force issues from within their organizations and the communities they serve, thus empowering leaders to ultimately use that information to achieve the gold standard of use of force management.

Symposium Planning/Advisory Group

January 5, 2010 (Alexandria, VA)

Steve Edwards
Corrections Senior Policy Advisor
Bureau of Justice Assistance

Betsy Gardner
Baltimore Liaison
Baltimore Mayor's Office

Joel H. Garner
Chief
Law Enforcement Statistics Unit
Bureau of Justice Statistics

Mary Gavin
Deputy Chief
Falls Church Police Department

Francis Healy
Lieutenant
Philadelphia Police Department

Steve Ijames
Major (ret.)
Springfield Police Department

Karen Kruger
Attorney
Funk & Bolton Attorneys at Law

Jessie Lee
Executive Director
National Organization of Black Law
Enforcement Executives

Bernard Melekian
Director
Office of Community Oriented
Policing Services

Colonel Frank Pawlowski
Commissioner
Pennsylvania State Police

Al Pearsall
*Special Assistant to the Principal
Deputy Director*
Office of Community Oriented
Policing Services

Ellen Scrivner
Deputy Director
National Institute of Justice

Sabrina Tapp-Harper
Major
Baltimore Police Department

Drew Tracy
Assistant Chief of Police
Montgomery County Police
Department

Jack Tucker
Lieutenant
Alameda County Sheriff's Office

Charles F. Wellford, Ph.D.
*Professor, Department of Criminology
and Criminal Justice*
University of Maryland–College Park

IACP Staff

Jim McMahon
*Chief of Staff, Deputy Executive
Director*

John Firman
Director of Research

David Paulson
*Administrator for Information and
Internet Technologies*

Aviva Kurash
Program Manager

William Sorukas
Chief Inspector
United States Marshal Service
IACP Fellow

Phil Lynn
Manager, Policy Center

Jenny Gargano
Project Assistant
National Law Enforcement Leadership
Initiative on Violence Against
Women

Andrew Corsoro
IT/Visual Information Tech

Use of Force Symposium Meeting Participants

May 4, 2011 (Alexandria, VA)

Geoffrey Alpert
Professor
University of South Carolina

Merrick Bobb
Director
Police Assessment Resource Center

Philip Broadfoot
Chief of Police
Danville Police Department

Michael Carroll
Chief of Police
West Goshen Police Department

Jack Collins, Esq.
Massachusetts Chiefs of Police
    Association

Justin Cuomo
Corporal
Falls Church Police Department

Louis Dekmar
Chief of Police
City of LaGrange

Nicole Dennis, J.D.
Program Specialist
Office of Community Oriented
    Policing Services

Joshua Ederheimer
Principal Deputy Director
Office of Community Oriented
    Policing Services

Philip Eure
President
Office of Police Complaints

Pete Evans
Major
Baltimore County Police Department

Joel H. Garner
Chief
Law Enforcement Statistics Unit
Bureau of Justice Statistics

Mary Gavin
Deputy Chief
Falls Church Police Department

David Giroux
Lieutenant
Arlington County Police Department

Steven Ijames
Major (Ret.)
Springfield Police Department

Matthew Klein
Commander
Metropolitan Police Department

Jessie Lee
Director
National Organization of Black Law
    Enforcement Executives

Daniel Longhurst
National Institute of Justice

Zenobia Mack-Burton
Detective
Metropolitan Police Department

Thomas Manger
Chief of Police
Montgomery County Police
    Department

Leonard Matarese
Director
International City/County
    Management Association

Genny May
United States Marshal Service

Kenneth McLaughlin
Chief of Police
Ocean View Police Department

Bernard Melekian
Director
Office of Community Oriented
    Policing Services

Todd Mercier
Sergeant
Metropolitan Police Department

Frank Pawlowski
Colonel (Ret.)
Pennsylvania State Police

Al Pearsall
*Special Assistant to the Principal
    Deputy Director*
Office of Community Oriented
    Policing Services

Adela Rivera
Commissioner
City of Detroit Board of Police
    Commissions

Dr. Andrew Ryan
Naval Criminal Investigative Service

Ellen Scrivner
Director
HIDTA, Office of National Drug Control
    Policy

Sabrina Tapp-Harper
Major
Baltimore Police Department

Arlinda Westbrook
Deputy Superintendent
New Orleans Police Department

IACP Staff

Daniel Rosenblatt
Executive Director

Jim McMahon
*Chief of Staff, Deputy Executive
    Director*

John Firman
Director of Research

David Paulson
*Administrator for Information and
    Internet Technologies*

Aviva Kurash
Program Manager

Lydia Blakey
Chief Inspector
United States Marshal Service
IACP Fellow

Scott Brien
Project Manager

Ian Hamilton
Project Manager

Carrie Corsoro
Research Center Coordinator

Jenny Gargano
Project Assistant
National Law Enforcement Leadership
    Initiative on Violence Against
    Women

Rochelle Love
Research Center Intern

Public perceptions of the use of force by law enforcement officers can dramatically and negatively affect the way the police and community interact. The International Association of Chiefs of Police (IACP) and the Office of Community Oriented Policing Services (COPS Office) convened a Use of Force Symposium to find ways in which law enforcement can address the perceived excessive use of force by officers. Discussions centered around five major themes, including public perception; getting at the facts; managing use of force; officer training; and officer mindset. *Emerging Use of Force Issues: Balancing Public and Officer Safety* summarizes the discussions from the Symposium and provides suggestions and conclusions on what actions can be taken to address these issues.

U.S. Department of Justice
Office of Community Oriented Policing Services
145 N Street, N.E.
Washington, DC 20530

To obtain details on COPS Office programs,
call the COPS Office Response Center at 800.421.6770

Visit **COPS** Online at www.cops.usdoj.gov.

e011226431
ISBN 978-1-935676-56-0
March 2012

9 781288 476037